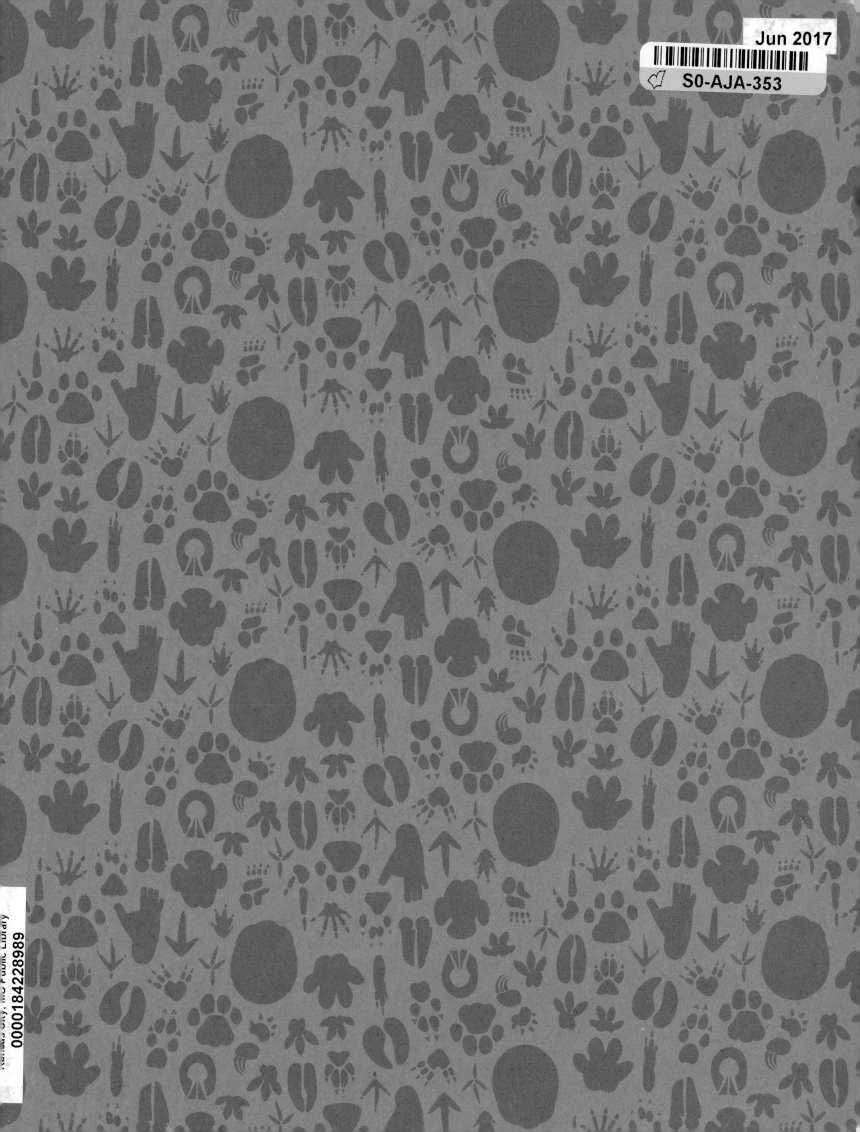

WILD ANIMALS OF THE SOUTH

Dieter Braun

Flying Eye Books
London - New York

THE WORLD OF WILD ANIMALS

There are many millions of animals in the world: mammals, birds, reptiles, fish, insects – no one quite knows how many actually populate our Earth. More are constantly being discovered and every year many disappear, never to be seen again. Even large and powerful animals like the tiger are threatened with extinction. Humankind could exist without tigers, tapirs or ocelots, but it would be wrong to assume that we are the most important creature on Earth. We are intruders in the animal kingdom and with every animal that dies out, our life on this planet loses a part of its power and colour and beauty. In fact, we don't want to even imagine a world without all of these amazing creatures that live in forests and jungles, in valleys and mountains, in oceans and savannahs, do we?

This book is dedicated to the animals in the southern half of the globe. It tells us how and where they live, what they look like, what they eat, how they find each other or hide from one another and all the other things they get up to. We'll take a look into hot, tropical corners, but also make a detour into the cold of the Antarctic, where life is especially hard but sometimes more peaceful – maybe because people don't show up there so often! No matter how different all of these animals are, how different their shapes, their colours or their way of life in the highest treetops, the deepest oceans or the starkest deserts, one thing ties them together: their will to live and their freedom.

Have fun in the wilderness!

AFRICA // REGION 1

SOUTH AMERICA // REGION 2

ASIA // *REGION 3*

AUSTRALIA // *REGION 4*

REGION 1
AFRICA

Ostrich // *Struthio camelus*

It is often said that ostriches stick their heads in the sand whenever danger is near, but in reality no one has ever seen this happen. The ostrich usually saves itself by running away at speeds of up to 70 kilometres an hour, or with a well-aimed kick. It has so much power in its huge feet that it can even put a big cat out of action. And beware: the male ostrich can roar like a lion!

White rhinoceros // *Ceratotherium simum*

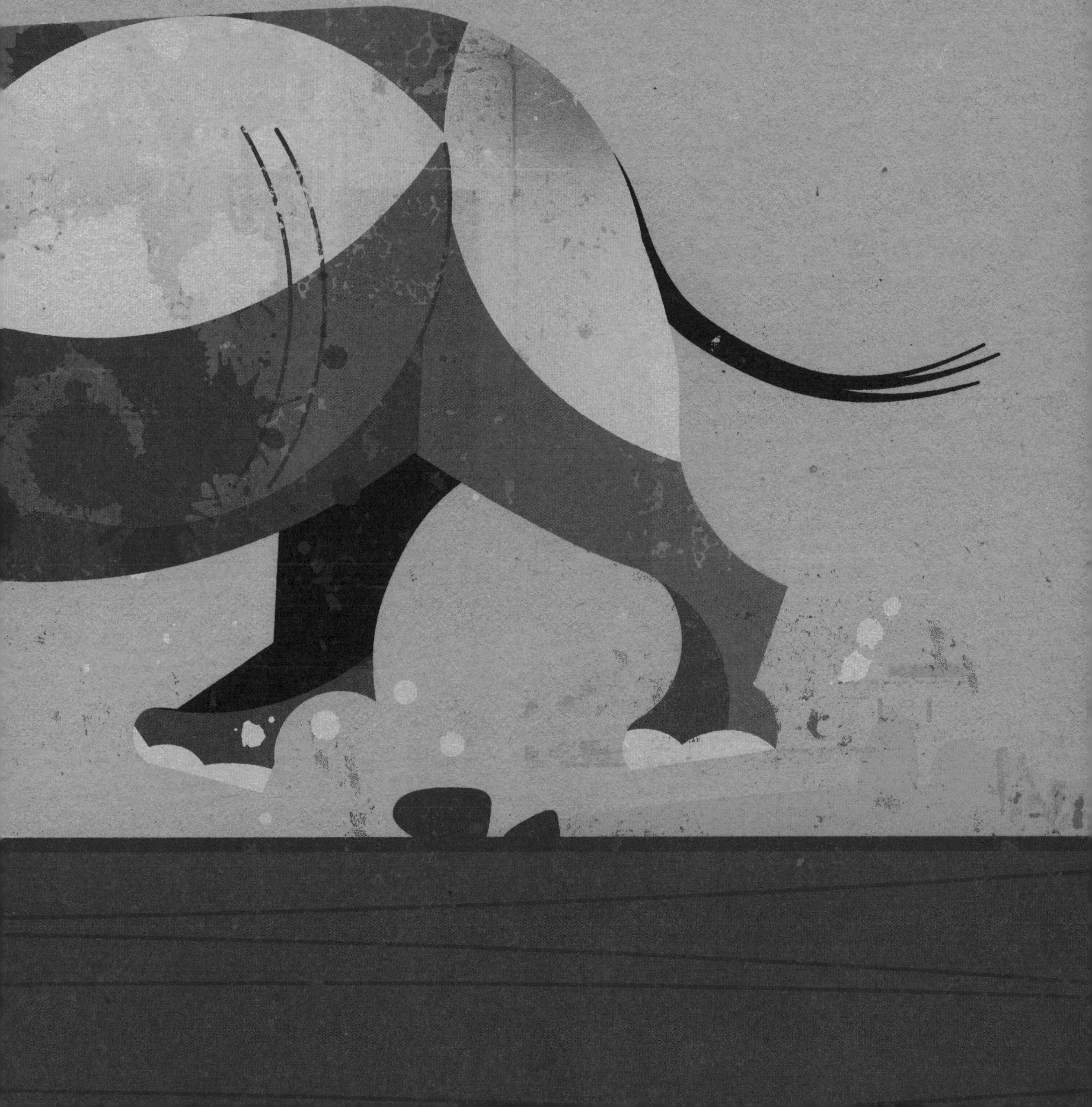

Lion // *Panthera leo*

The best thing about lions is their mane. The more nourished and strong a lion is, the darker, thicker and longer their mane appears. The females know this and prefer males with the most beautiful manes. And what do the other males do? They hold back whenever a fellow male with a more impressive hairstyle appears.

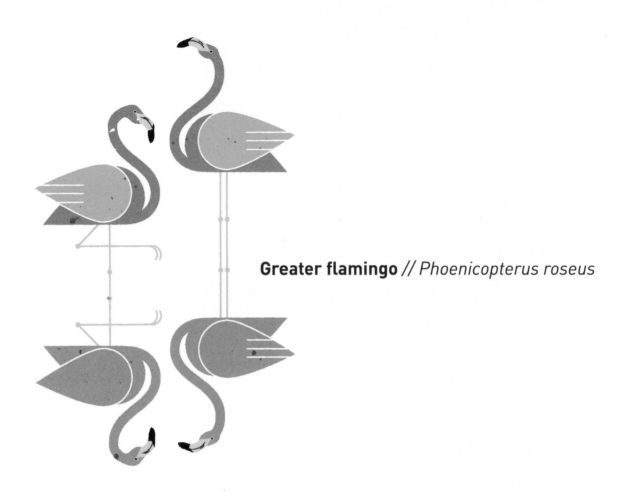

Greater flamingo // *Phoenicopterus roseus*

Hippopotamus // *Hippopotamus amphibius*

A typical day in the life of a hippopotamus looks something like this: sleep, rest, sleep, rest – and preferably while staying nice and comfortable in the water with only their nose, eyes and ears peeping out. Hippopotamuses aren't especially good swimmers, but they can run really fast for short periods. At night they forage for food on land, as they much prefer to eat grasses rather than aquatic plants.

White-backed vulture // *Gyps africanus*

Giraffe // *Giraffa camelopardalis*

Even though the giraffe's neck is over two metres
long, it only has seven vertebrae – just like humans.
In order to drink water, the giraffe must splay out
its legs and bow very deeply, but it has no problem
getting to the most delicious leaves in the highest
branches with its blue tongue. The scientific name
'camelopardalis' comes from the Greek words
for 'camel' and 'leopard', because it looks like
a mix between the two!

Mountain gorilla // *Gorilla beringei beringei*

Mountain gorillas have soft, black fur. When the males are fully grown at around 13 years old, the fur on their backs turns silver. Mountain gorillas live together in groups, always led by a strong silverback. The largest known group of gorillas are known as 'Pablo's', after their first silverback leader, and they have been elegantly walking on their knuckles through the borderlands between Rwanda, Uganda and the Congo for over 20 years.

East African oryx // *Oryx beisa*

Cheetah // *Acinonyx jubatus*

Cheetahs are the perfect sprinters. They have a long-legged and elegant body structure similar to a greyhound. Their paws have thick soles and their semi-retractable claws work like spikes – with the aid of these, they can run up to 110 kilometres an hour. Even though they reach a shoulder height of 80 centimetres, cheetahs aren't considered part of the big cat family. They don't roar like lions or leopards, but purr more like a cat.

African elephant // *Loxodonta africana*

The elephant is the largest living land mammal at over three metres tall and around 5,000 kilograms in weight. Their tusks can reach lengths of up to two and a half metres and their ears can be two metres long. As elephants can't sweat, they regulate their body temperature through their huge ears, and they also love to bathe. Elephants are strong swimmers and can stretch their trunk up like a snorkel out of the water.

Okapi // *Okapia johnstoni*

Leopard // *Panthera pardus*

Leopards are great climbers. They withdraw with their prey – which can weigh twice as much as they do – high up into the trees to be safe from enemies like lions and hyenas. This solitary creature doesn't even enjoy the company of its own kin. When it crosses paths with other leopards there is often a display of threatening behaviour that can lead to bloody fights.

Plains zebra // *Equus quagga*

Blue wildebeest // *Connochaetes taurinus*

These wildebeest live in the wide steppes and savannahs of southern and eastern Africa. They love to feed on grasses and weeds at dawn or in the cool of the evening, and the females live with their children in herds. The younger males that aren't yet strong enough to fight for the females roam in bachelor groups across the country – always careful to stay at a distance from the older males, who have their own territory.

Common chimpanzee // *Pan troglodytes*

Chimpanzees are very intelligent animals. They use stones and branches as tools and have their own language. When they speak to one another they are able to draw on a great range of sounds, but they can also make use of facial expressions and posture – and they can even laugh! The scientific name 'Pan' is a reference to the Greek god of nature and the wild.

Dik-dik // *Madoqua*

Mantled guereza // *Colobus guereza*

Mantis // *Mantodea*

The mantis is a master of disguise. Some look exactly the same colour and shape as dry branches, while others appear like long, green leaves. Their legs are equipped with spikes so that the mantis can grasp their prey securely. This can unfortunately also happen to the mantis itself – more often than not, the female will unceremoniously devour the male during mating.

Springbok // *Antidorcas marsupialis*

Greater kudu // *Tragelaphus strepsiceros*

Spotted hyena // *Crocuta crocuta*

Hyenas produce unbelievably strong digestive juices, which means that they can eat almost anything – from caterpillars to elephants, even bones, horns and hooves. They're like the vacuum cleaner of the savannah; perfect scavengers who like to make the most of what others leave behind. But there isn't only praise for the hyena: they are kleptoparasites, which means that they steal the freshly killed prey of other animals from right under their noses!

Warthog // *Phacochoerus africanus*

Sable antelope // *Hippotragus niger*

African wild dog // *Lycaon pictus*

Black-and-white ruffed lemur // *Varecia variegata*

Ring-tailed lemur // *Lemur catta*

These lemurs are exclusive to Madagascar. A typical group is comprised of 13 to 15 animals and is led by a dominant female. Even during fights within the group, the men usually draw the short straw and are placed at the back of the queue. Lemurs use their showy ringed tail in battle, which they use to wipe a secretion from their underarms and then swing towards their opponent.

Mandrill // *Mandrillus sphinx*

The mandrill is the most colourful of all mammals: blue and red on their face and bottom, olive green fur, a yellow beard and a white belly. This is a display of colour usually only found on birds, but mandrills live in the tropical rainforests of Central Africa after all, where everyone wears colour. The dominant males in the group develop the brightest tones on their face – you can recognise the head of the group by his snazzy blue cheeks.

Oxpecker // *Buphagus*

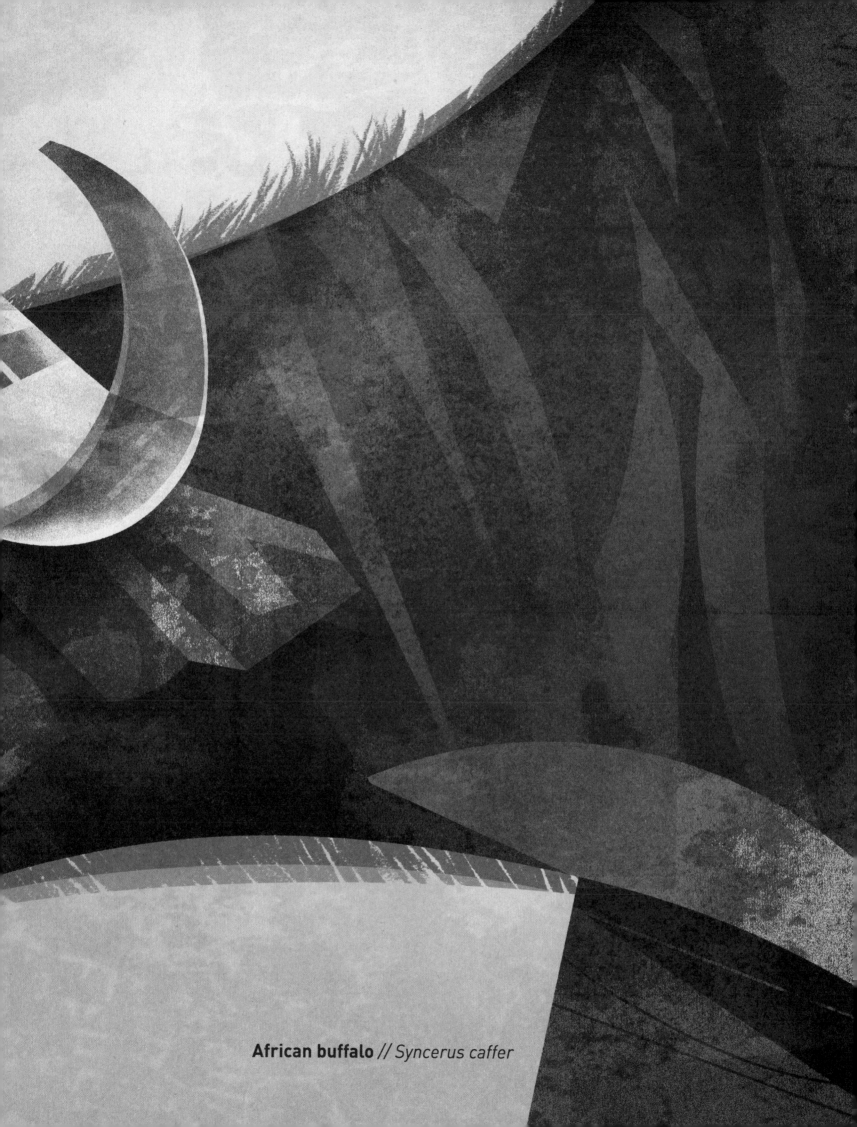

African buffalo // *Syncerus caffer*

REGION 2
SOUTH
AMERICA

Toco toucan // *Ramphastos toco*

The glowing yellow and red beak of the toco toucan is a kind of air conditioner. Through countless blood vessels in its beak, the bird releases heat and regulates its body temperature. Fully grown toucans are true masters of cooling down: they can precisely control how much heat they give out from 5% to 100%. And if the toucan gets too cold, it can insulate its beak under its wings to retain heat.

Capuchin // *Cebus*

Tamarin // *Saguinus*

Southern anteater // *Tamandua tetradactyla*

Giant anteater // *Myrmecophaga tridactyla*

The anteater's long, thin snout hides a 60 centimetre long sticky tongue. This is what it uses to fetch ants and termites – its favourite food – out of their nests. If it's not quick enough, the ants fight back and attack it with their acid, which can hurt the anteater in spite of its thick fur.

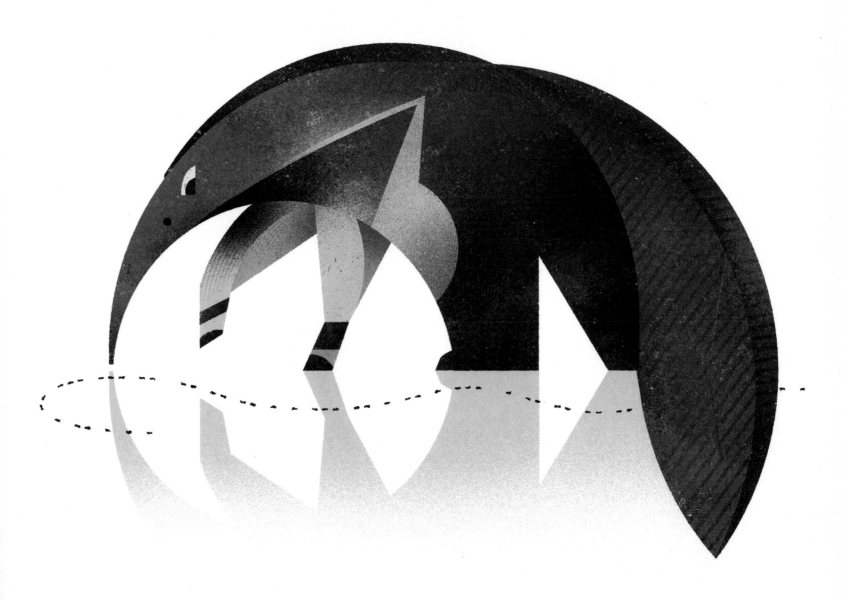

Squirrel monkey // *Saimiri*

Capybara // *Hydrochoerus hydrochaeris*

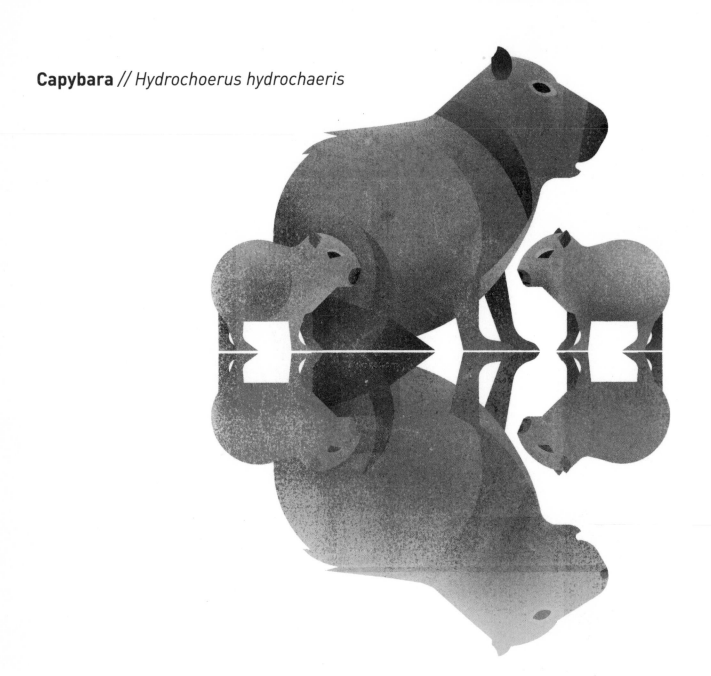

Maned wolf // *Chrysocyon brachyurus*

Red-haired like a fox, long-legged like a deer, and not actually a wolf – this maned canid is one good-looking animal! Its eponymous mane is mostly black and grows on its neck, muzzle and legs. The maned wolf is the largest wild dog in South America and is different to all its relatives on one point: it is solitary and doesn't live in a pack.

Two-toed sloth // *Choloepus*

Brown-throated sloth // *Bradypus variegatus*

As the sloth spends long periods of time hanging upside down from the tropical trees, this little animal's long fur is neatly parted on its belly to allow rain water to run off it more easily. Its fur shimmers green due to the algae that grows on it, acting both as camouflage and as a source of food for the sloth. The algae brings additional nourishment when leaves aren't enough – or when the sloth is just too lazy to move.

Jaguar // *Panthera onca*

The name of this animal comes from a Tupi-Guarani language of South America, meaning 'beast'. The jaguar likes to hunt near water and has the most powerful bite of all big cats. It can crack open a tortoise shell, or kill its prey with one quick, well-aimed bite to its cranium!

Galápagos tortoise // *Chelonoidis nigra*

Turquoise-browed motmot
// *Eumomota superciliosa*

Ocelot // *Leopardus pardalis*

Ocelots inhabit the whole of South America, but most of them live in the Amazon. They are nocturnal hunters, good climbers, solitary creatures, and mark important places with their urine. During the day, they spend their time sleeping in cosy places. They resolutely protect their territory and if a fellow creature crosses the border, they can expect a fight. Mice, birds and fish are on their menu – ocelots are real kitty cats.

Alpaca // *Vicugna pacos*

Alpacas are related to camels, which is why they are also called 'New World camels'. They are most happy in the company of their herd and on the high plateaus of the Andes. Their incredibly soft and lightweight fiber (similar to sheep's wool) isn't the only great thing about them – they also have a very peaceful nature. This is why alpacas can be used as therapy for people with mental illness – just being in contact with these cuddly animals with gentle eyes can ease tension.

Llama // *Lama glama*

Macaw // *Ara*

The macaw's beak is almost like a third foot. It uses it to climb and as a universal tool: from cracking shells and building nests, to feather maintenance and social bonding. Macaws are usually monogamous – once they have chosen a partner they stay together for the rest of their lives. And that can be a while: macaws can live for up to 60 years.

Nine-banded armadillo // *Dasypus novemcinctus*

The nine-banded armadillo is one of the noisier forest-dwellers. It lets out a wheezing grunt when digging holes or defending itself and squeals loudly if it's afraid. While foraging for food it snorts and grunts to itself and constantly snaps dry branches or kicks up leaves. These armadillos give birth to four genetically identical pups at a time – unique among mammals.

Giant otter // *Pteronura brasiliensis*

Poison dart frog // *Dendrobatidae*

REGION 3
ASIA

Bengal tiger // *Panthera tigris tigris*

The Bengal tiger is a powerful animal. From its muzzle to the tip of its tail it is easily three metres long, and the males can weigh up to 300 kilograms. The fur between its terrific stripes shimmers red and gold. A fully grown Bengal tiger can eat 30 kilograms of meat in one night – but it will only attack humans if it believes it needs to protect itself or its family.

Malayan tapir // *Tapirus indicus*

Little egret // *Egretta garzetta*

Large flying fox // *Pteropus vampyrus*

Lar gibbon // *Hylobates lar*

Lar gibbons, also known as white-handed gibbons, have extremely long arms which they use to elegantly swing from branch to branch. However, gibbons generally don't have a tail. They rarely step onto the forest floor, and why should they? They can find everything that their refined taste desires: ripe fruit, fresh leaves and tender buds. Now and again, they pick a bird right out of the air. The colour of their fur varies from black and brown to sandy and yellow.

Asian elephant // *Elephas maximus*

Indian rhinoceros // *Rhinoceros unicornis*

In German, the Indian rhinoceros is called a 'shell rhinoceros' due to the thick flaps of skin that cover its massive body, making it appear as if it has a heavy shell strapped to its back. Although these powerful animals look rather cumbersome, they are surprisingly nimble runners – they can accelerate their 2000 kilogram body to speeds of up to 55 kilometres an hour! On top of that, they are good swimmers and love wallowing in mud. Unlike their African relatives, they only have one horn.

Great hornbill // *Buceros bicornis*

Common kingfisher
// *Alcedo atthis*

Indian peafowl // *Pavo cristatus*

A real eye-catcher! The most striking feature of the Indian peafowl is its plumage. The male peafowl, or peacock, has an elongated train comprising of more than 200 decorative feathers ending in bright eyespots. Using this elaborate display, the males try and attract female peahens during courtship. The peafowl is highly prized in India, as they frighten away poisonous cobras and warn when tigers are coming with their shrill cries.

REGION 4
AUSTRALIA

Galah // *Eolophus roseicapilla*

The rose-breasted cockatoo, or galah, is an acrobat of the skies. Able to reach speeds of 70 kilometres an hour with playful twists and turns in flight, it proves itself to be more skilled than all the other kinds of cockatoo. This striking pink and grey parrot thrives in hot and arid regions as well as wetter areas of the Australian continent.

Saltwater crocodile // *Crocodylus porosus*

Known as the saltwater crocodile, this gigantic Indo-Pacific crocodile can actually live in both fresh and salt water. You'll find it in rivers and swamps inland and in coastal areas of the oceans, but there have also been instances of them being 1000 kilometres away from land out on the high seas. The small, young crocodiles are hunted by birds of prey or carnivorous fish – when fully grown, however, they have no natural predators and can live for up to 70 years.

Koala // *Phascolarctos cinereus*

Koalas are often called koala bears, but they're not bears at all – they are marsupials. You will usually find koalas sleeping in the branches of a eucalyptus tree. With their daily dose of 20 hours of sleep, these little creatures out-sleep even the sloth. Koalas need so much sleep because they don't get a lot of energy from their main source of food – eucalyptus leaves. These leaves are highly poisonous to humans, but for koalas there is nothing more delicious. Well then, bon appétit!

Common wombat // *Vombatus ursinus*

The common wombat is the teddy bear of Australia. Its short legs, stocky body and rounded ears only add to its cuddly appearance. Especially striking is its hairless snout, which earned it the nickname 'bare-nosed'. Good luck trying to see a wombat in the wild – these marsupials only come out in the evening or at night and happily sleep away the day in their burrows.

Tasmanian devil // *Sarcophilus harrisii*

The Tasmanian devil is the largest carnivorous marsupial in Australia, but it now only exists on the island of Tasmania. It got its name from the early European settlers, who feared that the creature was some sort of unholy beast due to its pitch-black fur, glowing red ears, and harsh shriek. Every now and again the Tasmanian devil will hunt small rodents and birds, but it mostly eats carrion. This is why it's often described as the 'vacuum cleaner of the forest'.

Red kangaroo // *Macropus rufus*

Alongside koalas, many people associate the Australian animal kingdom with kangaroos. The greatest specimen of this species and the largest marsupial in the world is the red kangaroo. Males can be up to 1.6 metres tall and 55 to 90 kilograms in weight. With a physique like that, you had better not mess with them – these giants are excellent boxers. Their kick-boxing technique mostly comes in use when fighting over a mate.

Common spotted cuscus
// Spilocuscus maculatus

Echidna *// Tachyglossidae*

Tree-kangaroo // *Dendrolagus*

Laughing kookaburra // *Dacelo novaeguineae*

The laughing kookaburra – also known as 'laughing jack' – belongs to the kingfisher family and predominantly lives in Australia. The bird gets its name from the raucous cackling sound it uses to defend its territory. Often heard in the early mornings and late evenings, the laughing kookaburra's distinctive call has given it the nickname 'bushman's clock'. 'Kookaburra' is a well-loved children's song in Australia.

Dugong // *Dugong dugon*

Dingo // *Canis lupus dingo*

Australian white ibis // *Threskiornis moluccus*

The Australian white ibis loves to feed on meat. At the top of the menu are mussels and crustaceans, which is why it stays close to water. With its long, powerful beak it pokes around in marshy, shallow water to pick out the best titbits.

Frilled-neck lizard // *Chlamydosaurus kingii*

The frilled-neck lizard's defining quality, as its name suggests, is the ruff of skin on its neck that can unfold like an umbrella. It doesn't use this to protect itself from rain, but rather to frighten its enemies or communicate with peers. With its ruff puffed out, it resembles a little dragon. When this display doesn't work, the frilled-neck lizard jumps up onto its hind legs and runs at lightning speed to the nearest tree.

Victoria crowned pigeon // *Goura victoria*

Frogmouth // *Podargidae*

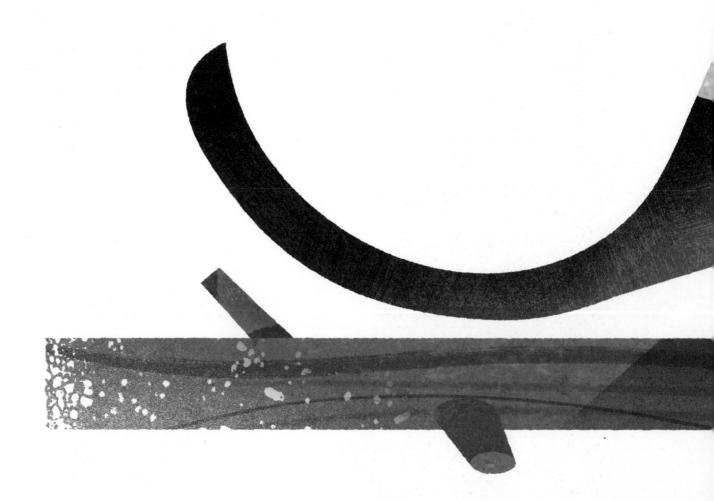

Numbat // *Myrmecobius fasciatus*

Another Australian marsupial is the numbat, also known as the banded anteater. Unlike other marsupials, the numbat doesn't have a pouch for its young and it hunts for insects during the daytime rather than in the night. The numbat mostly eats termites and ants and laps them up with its long tongue, which is around 10 centimetres long – almost a third of the length of the whole animal.

Emu // *Dromaius novaehollandiae*

Southern cassowary // *Casuarius casuarius*

REGION 5
ANTARCTICA

Southern elephant seal // *Mirounga leonina*

Kelp gull // *Larus dominicanus*

Leopard seal // *Hydrurga leptonyx*

The leopard seal is to be treated with caution! Penguins, birds, krill, crustaceans, and even other seals need to be wary when this mighty predator is hungry. If the leopard seal stays out of the way of its only natural predator – the orca – it can live for up to 26 years.

Chinstrap penguin // *Pygoscelis antarctica*

Adélie penguin // *Pygoscelis adeliae*

Gentoo penguin // *Pygoscelis papua*

Emperor penguin // *Aptenodytes forsteri*

When it comes to surviving in the Antarctic, emperor penguins stick together. Huddled in large, tightly packed groups, the penguins take turns entering the warm centre to shelter from the freezing winds outside. In order to keep the chicks especially cosy, the eggs are kept inside a so-called brood pouch – the father's, that is. The mother lays only one egg per year, then returns to the sea for two months. Upon her return, she finds the father through his unique call and feeds the newly hatched chick with partially digested fish.

Humpback whale // *Megaptera novaeangliae*

When a humpback whale dives, it first bends its back into a hump – hence the name – and then lifts its tail completely out of the water. The tail of each whale is completely unique, just like a fingerprint. Humpback whales are also known for their acrobatic leaps out of the water and their ethereal songs, which can last for an entire day and night. The males use these to try to attract females during mating season. A humpback whale can weigh up to 30 tonnes, or as much as six adult African elephants.

INDEX
AFRICA // *Region 1*

Ostrich
Struthio camelus // p. 8

White rhinoceros
Ceratotherium simum // p. 10

Lion
Panthera leo // p. 12

Greater flamingo
Phoenicopterus roseus // p. 14

Hippopotamus
Hippopotamus amphibius // p. 14

White-backed vulture
Gyps africanus // p. 16

Giraffe
Giraffa camelopardalis // p. 18

Mountain gorilla
Gorilla beringei beringei // p. 20

East African oryx
Oryx beisa // p. 22

Cheetah
Acinonyx jubatus // p. 24

African elephant
Loxodonta africana // p. 26

Okapi
Okapia johnstoni // p. 28

Leopard
Panthera pardus // p. 30

Blue wildebeest
Connochaetes taurinus // p. 32

Plains zebra
Equus quagga // p. 33

Common chimpanzee
Pan troglodytes // p. 34

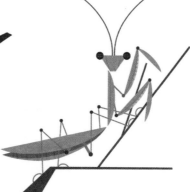

Dik-dik
Madoqua // p. 36

Mantled guereza
Colobus guereza // p. 37

Mantis
Mantodea // p. 38

Greater kudu
Tragelaphus strepsiceros // p. 40

Springbok
Antidorcas marsupialis // p. 41

Spotted hyena
Crocuta crocuta // p. 42

Warthog
Phacochoerus africanus // p. 44

Sable antelope
Hippotragus niger // p. 45

African wild dog
Lycaon pictus // p. 46

Ring-tailed lemur
Lemur catta // p. 48

**Black-and-white
ruffed lemur**
Varecia variegata // p. 49

Oxpecker
Buphagus // p. 52

Mandrill
Mandrillus sphinx // p. 50

African buffalo
Syncerus caffer // p. 52

Toco toucan
Ramphastos toco // p. 56

Tamarin
Saguinus // p. 58

Capuchin
Cebus // p. 59

Southern anteater
Tamandua tetradactyla // p. 60

Giant anteater
Myrmecophaga tridactyla // p. 61

Squirrel monkey
Saimiri // p. 62

Hummingbird
Trochilidae // p. 63

Capybara
Hydrochoerus hydrochaeris // p. 64

Maned wolf
Chrysocyon brachyurus // p. 65

Brown-throated sloth
Bradypus variegatus // p. 66

Two-toed sloth
Choloepus // p. 67

Galápagos tortoise
Chelonoidis nigra // p. 68

Jaguar
Panthera onca // p. 69

Ocelot
Leopardus pardalis // p. 70

Turquoise-browed motmot
Eumomota superciliosa // p. 71

Llama
Lama glama // p. 73

Macaw
Ara // p. 74

Alpaca
Vicugna pacos // p. 72

Nine-banded armadillo
Dasypus novemcinctus // p. 76

Giant otter
Pteronura brasiliensis // p. 77

Poison dart frog
Dendrobatidae // p. 78

Bengal tiger
Panthera tigris tigris // p. 82

Malayan tapir
Tapirus indicus // p. 84

Little egret
Egretta garzetta // p. 86

Lar gibbon
Hylobates lar // p. 88

Large flying fox
Pteropus vampyrus // p. 89

Asian elephant
Elephas maximus // p. 90

Indian rhinoceros
Rhinoceros unicornis // p. 92

Great hornbill
Buceros bicornis // p. 93

Common kingfisher
Alcedo atthis // p. 94

Indian peafowl
Pavo cristatus // p. 96

Galah
Eolophus roseicapilla // p. 100

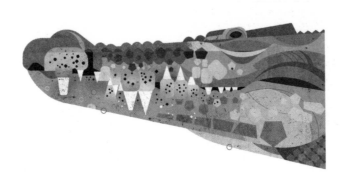

Saltwater crocodile
Crocodylus porosus // p. 102

Koala
Phascolarctos cinereus // p. 104

Common wombat
Vombatus ursinus // p. 106

Tasmanian devil
Sarcophilus harrisii // p. 107

Red kangaroo
Macropus rufus // p. 108

Common spotted cuscus
Spilocuscus maculatus // p. 110

Echidna
Tachyglossidae // p. 110

Tree-kangaroo
Dendrolagus // p. 111

Laughing kookaburra
Dacelo novaeguineae // p. 112

Dugong
Dugong dugon // p. 113

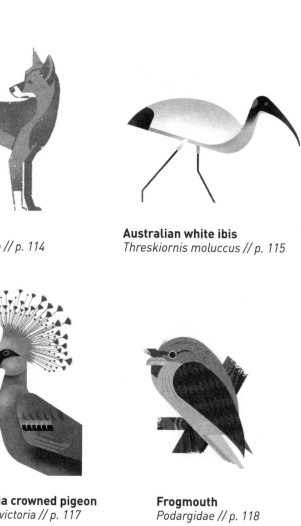

Dingo
Canis lupus dingo // p. 114

Australian white ibis
Threskiornis moluccus // p. 115

Frilled-neck lizard
Chlamydosaurus kingii // p. 116

Victoria crowned pigeon
Goura victoria // p. 117

Frogmouth
Podargidae // p. 118

Numbat
Myrmecobius fasciatus // p. 119

Southern cassowary
Casuarius casuarius // p. 120

Emu
Dromaius novaehollandiae // p. 121

ANTARCTICA // *Region 5*

Kelp gull
Larus dominicanus // p. 124

Southern elephant seal
Mirounga leonina // p. 125

Leopard seal
Hydrurga leptonyx // p. 126

Adélie penguin
Pygoscelis adeliae // p. 127

Chinstrap penguin
Pygoscelis antarctica // p. 127

Gentoo penguin
Pygoscelis papua // p. 127

Emperor penguin
Aptenodytes forsteri // p. 128

Humpback whale
Megaptera novaeangliae // p. 130

With special thanks to Simone Buchholz, Adriane Krakowski and Judith Schüller.
I would go on safari with you.

This is a first English edition.

Published in 2017 by Flying Eye Books, an imprint of Nobrow Ltd.
27 Westgate Street, London E8 3RL.

Text and illustrations © 2014 Dieter Braun.

This edition is published under licence from Knesebeck GmbH & Co.
Verlag KG, München. Ein Unternehmen der La Martinière Groupe.
All rights reserved.

Translation by Jen Calleja.

Published in the US by Nobrow (US) Inc.
Printed in Latvia on FSC® certified paper

MIX
Paper from
responsible sources
FSC® C002795

ISBN: 978-1-909263-97-0
Order from www.flyingeyebooks.com

Also available:
Wild Animals of the North
by Dieter Braun
ISBN: 978-1-909263-96-3

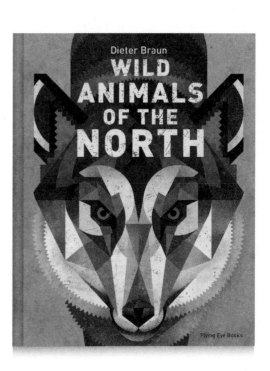